© 2002 by Barbour Publishing, Inc.

ISBN 1-58660-463-5

Cover Image © Getty One

Viola Ruelke Gommer contributed to the selections on pp. 10-13, 18-19, 33, and 35-36.

Published by Barbour Books, an imprint of Barbour Publishing, Inc., P.O. Box 719, Uhrichsville, Ohio 44683, www.barbourbooks.com

Member of the
Evangelical Christian
Publishers Association

Printed in China.
5 4 3 2 1

Be Encouraged

Ellyn Sanna

DayMaker
GREETING BOOKS

I am thinking of you today,
saying a prayer
that you might take heart,
gather strength,
and be inspired
to face your life with new energy.

May you be encouraged. . .

When You Are Afraid
When You Are Overwhelmed
When You Are Sorrowing
When Life Seems Hopeless

I have. . .
learned that when a baffling or painful experience comes,
the crucial thing is not always to find the right answers,
but to ask the right questions. . . .
Often it is simply the right question at the right time
that propels us into the journey of awakening.

Sue Monk Kidd

I know how hard your life is right now.
I am praying that God will encourage you
and transform this difficult time
into a " journey of awakening."

I

When You Are Afraid

The word *courage* comes from the Latin word for *heart*—
and courage is born in the heart.
Courageous acts come from the heart.
And a courageous life is lived from the heart.
So live your life from your heart,
and you will find the courage you need entwined in your living.

*Courage is the capacity to go ahead
in spite of the fear.*

SCOTT PECK

*Character cannot be developed in ease and quiet.
Only through experience of trial and suffering
can the soul be strengthened, vision cleared,
ambition inspired, and success achieved.*

HELEN KELLER

*Have confidence in God's mercy,
for when you think
He is a long way from you,
He is often quite near.*

THOMAS À KEMPIS

There is so much unknown in our lives;
it is only natural to feel frightened.
Like an animal caught in the headlights of oncoming doom,
we stand frozen, staring helplessly,
trying to see the path ahead before we dare to take a step,
and all the while, life rushes at us. . . .
When you find yourself terrified, ask,
"What should I do?"
the answer is far more simple than you think.

Your heart is beating with God's love;
open it to others.
He has entrusted you with gifts and talents;
use them for His service.
He goes before you each step of the way;
walk in faith.
Take courage.
Step out into the unknown
with the One who knows all.

To encourage means to:

Strengthen
Fortify
Inspire
Cheer
Nourish
Nudge
Reassure

I will be there to help you face your fears.
God has already provided all you need.
Let me help you find courage.
It is there waiting—
deep inside you,
put there by the One who loves you—
but your fear is blinding you.

You are my hiding place;
you will protect me from trouble
and surround me with songs of deliverance.

PSALM 32:7

When fear fills your heart,
may you hear God's song of deliverance
and be encouraged.

14

II

When You Are Overwhelmed

It is difficulties that show what people are.

EPICURUS

A burden, even a small one,
when carried alone and in isolation can destroy us,
but a burden when carried as part of God's burden
can lead us to new life.
That is the great mystery of our faith.

HENRI NOUWEN

As a young girl, my daughter often struggled with the experiences that came her way. At bedtime, we always talked about the particular struggles or problems she had faced that day. Our conversations usually led us to the conclusion that she could grow strong in character as she dealt with each day's problems. What looked like problems were really chances for her to grow.

But one day she came home from school obviously frustrated and overwhelmed. When I asked her what was wrong, her answer was loud and immediate:

"I'm tired of these character-building experiences!"

We all have those moments. We're only human—and we do get tired. But as an adult, my daughter is truly strong of character. God used her difficult times to help create the woman she is today. And He will do the same for you and me.

VIOLA RUELKE GOMMER

Hearty through hardship.

GEORGE MACDONALD

*"Everything is possible
for him who believes."*

MARK 9:23

You may think you cannot make it through one more day.
Struggles, hardships, pain, and difficulty envelop you.
You cry out (to God, to life),
"Please. No more! I can't endure anything else."
Ask yourself: *Can I make it through the next hour?*
If so, put your energy into that, and no more.
If you can't make it through the next hour,
can you endure the next half hour. . .
the next fifteen minutes. . .
the next minute?

Then commit yourself to that small space of time
and look no farther ahead.
Take hours, minutes, and moments as they come,
one at a time.
Don't run ahead.
Do what you can now. . .
and at the end of the day, let it go.
Put all that is left undone in God's hands.
God is at work in ways you cannot see.
Trust Him.
Sleep. . .rest. . .
Relax in His arms.

*Have courage for the great sorrows of life
and patience for the small ones;
and when you have laboriously accomplished your daily tasks,
go to sleep in peace. God is awake.*

VICTOR HUGO

*Let him have all your worries and cares,
for he is always thinking about you
and watching everything that concerns you.*

1 PETER 5:7 TLB

Each dawn holds a new hope
for a new plan,
making the start of each day
the start of a new life.

GINA BLAIR

Wake each morning with a sense of hope.
God has amazing things in store for you.
And He does all things well.

*R*esolve to see the world on the sunny side,
and you have almost won the battle of life at the outset.

SIR ROGER L'ESTRANGE

*It is not what happens that matters,
but how you take it.*

HANS SELYE

*T*ake your everyday, ordinary life—
your sleeping, eating, going-to-work, and walking-around life—
and place it before God as an offering.

ROMANS 12:1 *THE MESSAGE*

To be glad of life, because it gives you the chance to love
and to work and to play and to look up at the stars; . . .
to think. . .everyday of Christ;
and to spend as much time as you can,
with body and with spirit, in God's out-of-doors—
these are little guideposts on the footpath to peace.

HENRY VAN DYKE

*May you follow God's footpath
all the way home to His peace.*

Every spirit builds itself a house,
and beyond its house a world,
and beyond its world a heaven.
Know then that world exists for you.

RALPH WALDO EMERSON

We need time to dream, time to remember,
and time to reach the infinite.
Time to be.

GLADYS TABER

Don't get so busy that you forget to simply *be*.
Sometimes the best way to stop being overwhelmed by life
is to simply step back,
take a day. . .or an hour. . .or a moment,
and notice all that God is doing in your life.

When we take time to notice the simple things in life,
we never lack for encouragement.
We discover we are surrounded by limitless hope
that's just wearing everyday clothes.

ANONYMOUS

III

When You Are Sorrowing

Each of us may be sure that if God sends us on stony paths
He will provide us with strong shoes,
and He will not send us out on any journey
for which He does not equip us well.

ALEXANDER MACLAREN

I know how much you're hurting right now.
If I could, I'd take the pain away.
But I can't.
So instead I'm praying that God will provide you
with "heart-shoes" strong enough
to withstand even the sharpest stones.

*The Lord's mercy often rides
to the door of our heart
upon the black horse of affliction.*

CHARLES SPURGEON

Our life is full of brokenness—broken relationships,
broken promises, broken expectations.
How can we live with that brokenness
without becoming bitter and resentful
except by returning again and again
to God's faithful presence in our lives?

HENRI NOUWEN

I am the man who has seen affliction. . . .
He pierced my heart. . . .
I have been deprived of peace;
I have forgotten what prosperity is.
So I say, "My splendor is gone
and all that I had hoped from the Lord". . . .
My soul is downcast within me.
Yet this I call to mind
and therefore I have hope:

Because of the Lord's great love we are not consumed,
for his compassions never fail.
They are new every morning;
great is your faithfulness.
I say to myself, "The Lord is my portion;
therefore I will wait for him."
The Lord is good to those whose hope is in him,
to the one who seeks him;
it is good to wait quietly
for the salvation of the Lord.

LAMENTATIONS 3:1, 13, 17–18, 20–26

When life hurts,
God shows us He cares
through one another.
I am here for you.
I care.

IV

When You Are Discouraged

Our greatest glory consists not in never falling,
but in rising every time we fall.

OLIVER GOLDSMITH

*Don't let life discourage you;
everyone who got where he is
had to begin where he was.*

ROGER L. EVANS

When we face the worst that can happen
in any situation, we grow.
When circumstances are at their worst,
we can find our best.

ELIZABETH KUBLER-ROSS & DAVID KESSLER

*B*e encouraged—
    for the Giver of Good Things,
      the Renewer of Hope,
        and the Dispenser of Wonderful Surprises
        is on your side.
He loves you. . .and He never fails.

*Still round the corner there may wait,
a new road, or a secret gate.*

J. R. R. TOLKIEN

*B*ecause we are often spiritually blind,
we fail to see God's hand at work.
God is there, though, present where we least expect Him.
My prayer is that God will surprise you today.
In your daily routine, in the stressful details of ordinary life,
when you least expect it,
may grace leap out at you,
encouraging your heart.

He restores my soul.

PSALM 23:3

Never think that God's delays
are God's denials.
Hold on; hold fast; hold out.
Patience is genius.

COMTE DE BUFFON

Even when you are discouraged,
hold on to your dreams.
They have no expiration date.

When difficulties and disappointments come my way, I ask myself two questions:

How can this be used for good?

and

What is the lesson in this for me?

Of course, I always ask a third question as well:

Why me?

But there is really no answer to that question. So I go back to the first two questions. They help me accept the situation; they show me the positive side; they direct me toward concrete action. Most of all, they help me to move on.

VIOLA RUELKE GOMMER

*E*verything we call a trial, a sorrow, or a duty,
believe me, that an angel's hand is there.

FRA GIOVANNI

*M*ay you see the angels' hands
at work in your life!

*G*od may be invisible, but He's in touch.
You may not be able to see Him,
but He is in control. . . .
That includes all of life—past, present, future.

CHARLES SWINDOLL

*If we had no winter,
the spring would not be so pleasant:
if we did not sometimes taste adversity,
prosperity would not be so welcome.*

ANNE BRADSTREET

Even in the winter, even in the midst of the storm,
the sun is still there. Somewhere, up above the clouds,
it still shines and warms and pulls at the life
buried deep inside the brown branches and frozen earth.
The sun is there! Spring will come!
The clouds cannot stay forever.

GLORIA GAITHER

Be Encouraged

God came to us because God wanted to join us on the road,
to listen to our story, and to help us realize
that we are not walking in circles
but moving toward the house of peace and joy.

THOMAS MERTON

When your way seems long and hard,
and you are tempted to give up,
remember:
You are not alone.
Jesus is walking at your side.
Trust Him to lead you home
to everlasting peace and joy.

*How great is the love
the Father has lavished on us,
that we should be called children of God!
And that is what we are!*

1 JOHN 3:1

*May your life become one of
glad and unending praise to the Lord
as you journey through this world,
and in the world that is to come!*

TERESA OF AVILA

Be Encouraged!